Starting with... Role play

Ourselves

Diana Bentley
Maggie Hutchings
Dee Reid

Diana Bentley is an educational consultant for primary literacy and has written extensively for both teachers and children. She worked for many years in the Centre for the Teaching of Reading at Reading University and then became a Senior Lecturer in Primary English at Oxford Brookes University. Throughout her professional life she has continued to work in schools and teach children aged from 5 to 11 years.

Maggie Hutchings has considerable experience teaching KS1 and Early Years. She is a Leading Teacher for literacy in The Foundation Stage and is a Foundation Stage and Art coordinator. Maggie is passionate about the importance of learning through play and that learning should be an exciting and fun experience for young children. Her school's art work has been exhibited in The National Gallery, London.

Dee Reid is a former teacher who has been an independent consultant in primary literacy for over 20 years in many local authorities. She is consultant to 'Catch Up' – a special needs literacy intervention programme used in over 4,000 schools in the UK. She is Series Consultant to 'Storyworlds' (Heinemann) and her recent publications include 'Think About It' (Nelson Thornes) and Literacy World (Heinemann).

Other titles in the series:

Colour and light
Under the ground
Emergency 999
Into space
At the hospital
Fairytales
At the garage/At the airport
All creatures great and small
On the farm
Water

Other Foundation titles:

Starting with stories and poems:

Self esteem
Self care
A sense of community
Making relationships
Behaviour and self control

A collection of stories and poems

The authors would like to thank Jane Whitwell for all her hard work in compiling the resources and poems for the series.

Published by
Hopscotch Educational Publishing Ltd, Unit 2, The Old Brushworks, 56 Pickwick Road, Corsham, Wiltshire,
SN13 9BX
Tel: 01249 701701

© 2006 Hopscotch Educational Publishing

Written by Diana Bentley, Maggie Hutchings and Dee Reid
Series design by Blade Communications
Cover illustration by Sami Sweeten
Illustrated by Susan Hutchison
Printed by Colorman (Ireland) Ltd

ISBN 1 905390 10 6

Diana Bentley, Maggie Hutchings and Dee Reid hereby assert their moral right to be identified as the authors of this work in accordance with the Copyright, Designs and Patents Act, 1988.

The authors and publisher would like to thank Chapter One (a specialist children's book shop) in Wokingham for all their help and support. Email: chapteronebookshop@yahoo.co.uk

All rights reserved. This book is sold subject to the condition that it shall not, by way of trade or otherwise, be lent, hired out or otherwise circulated without the publisher's prior consent in any form of binding or cover other than that in which it is published and without a similar condition, including this condition, being imposed upon the subsequent purchaser.

No part of this publication may be reproduced, stored in a retrieval system, or transmitted, in any form or by any means, electronic, mechanical, photocopying, recording or otherwise, without the prior permission of the publisher, except where photocopying for educational purposes within the school or other educational establishment that has purchased this book is expressly permitted in the text.

Contents

Introduction	4
'Ourselves' planning chart	6
Week 1 – The nursery	7
Week 2 – Me, my family and friends	12
Week 3 – Emotions and feelings	16
Week 4 – Taste and smell in the kitchen	20
Week 5 – Sight and sounds in the kitchen	24
Week 6 – Touch	29
Photocopiables	33

Acknowledgements

The authors and publisher gratefully acknowledge permission to reproduce copyright material in this book.

'My brother' by Theresa Heine from *Twinkle Twinkle Chocolate Bar* compiled by John Foster (Oxford University Press) © 1994 Theresa Heine. Reproduced by kind permission of the author.

'Oh Baby!' by June Crebbin from *The Dinosaur's Dinner* (Viking) © June Crebbin. Reproduced by kind permission of the author.

'Potty, but True' reproduced by kind permission of The Agency (London) Ltd. Potty, but True © Tony Bradman 1984.

'Tiny Little Fingernails' Lyrics by Niki Davies © 1998 International Music Publications. Reproduced by permission of International Music Publications Ltd. All rights reserved.

'The Wrong Trolley' by Eric Finney from *An Orange Poetry Paintbox*, compiled by John Foster (Oxford University Press) © 1996 Eric Finney. Reproduced by kind permission of the author.

Every effort has been made to trace the owners of copyright of material in this book and the publisher apologises for any inadvertent omissions. Any persons claiming copyright for any material should contact the publisher who will be happy to pay the permission fees agreed between them and who will amend the information in this book on any subsequent reprint.

Introduction

There are 12 books in the series *Starting with role play* offering a complete curriculum for the Early Years.

Ourselves	At the garage/At the airport
Into space	Emergency 999
At the shops	All creatures great and small
Colour and light	Under the ground
At the hospital	Fairytales
On the farm	Water

While each topic is presented as a six-week unit of work, it can easily be adapted to run for fewer weeks if necessary. The themes have been carefully selected to appeal to boys and girls and to a range of cultural groups.

 Each unit addresses all six areas of learning outlined in the *Curriculum Guidance for the Foundation Stage* and the specific Early Learning Goal is identified for each activity and indicated by this symbol.

Generally, differentiation is achieved by outcome, although for some of the Communication, Language and Literacy strands and Mathematical Development strands, extension activities are suggested for older or more confident learners.

Suggested teaching sequence for each unit

Each week has been organised into a suggested teaching sequence. However, each activity in an area of learning links to other activities and there will be overlap as groups engage with the tasks.

The Core Curriculum: Literacy and Mathematics

Every school will have its own programmes for literacy and mathematics and it is not intended that the activities in the units in this book should replace these. Rather, the activities suggested aim to support any programme, to help to consolidate the learning and to demonstrate how the learning can be used in practical situations.

The importance of role play

'Children try out their most recent learning, skills and competences when they play. They seem to celebrate what they know.'

Tina Bruce (2001) *Learning Through Play: Babies, Toddlers and the Foundation Years*. London: Hodder & Stoughton.

Early Years practitioners are aware of the importance of play as a vehicle for learning. When this play is carefully structured and managed then the learning opportunities are greatly increased. Adult participation can be the catalyst for children's imaginations and creativity.

Six weeks allows for a role play area to be created, developed and expanded and is the optimum time for inspiring children and holding their interest. It is important not to be too prescriptive in the role play area. Teachers should allow for children's ideas and interests to evolve and allow time for the children to explore and absorb information. Sometimes, the children will take the topic off at a tangent or go into much greater depth than expected or even imagined.

Organising the classroom

The role play area could be created by partitioning off a corner of the classroom with ceiling drapes, an old-style clothes-horse, chairs, boxes, large-scale construction blocks (for example, 'Quadro') or even an open-fronted beach tent/shelter. Alternatively, the whole classroom could be dedicated to the role play theme.

Involving parents and carers

Encourage the children to talk about the topic and what they are learning with their parents or carers at home. With adult help and supervision, they can explore the internet and search for pictures in magazines and books. This enriches the learning taking place in the classroom.

Outside activities

The outdoor classroom should be an extension of the indoor classroom and it should support and enhance the activities offered inside. Boys, in particular, often feel less restricted in outdoor play. They may use language more purposefully and may even engage more willingly in reading and writing activities. In the

Introduction

outdoor area things can be done on a much bigger, bolder and noisier scale and this may connect with boys' preferred learning styles.

Observation in Salford schools and settings noted that boys access books much more readily when there is a book area outdoors.

Resources

Role play areas can be more convincing reconstructions when they are stocked with authentic items. Car boot sales, jumble sales and charity shops are good sources of artefacts. It is a good idea to inform parents and carers of topics well in advance so they can be looking out for objects and materials that will enhance the role play area.

Reading

Every week there should be a range of opportunities for children to participate in reading experiences. These should include:

Shared reading

The practitioner should read aloud to the children from Big Books, modelling the reading process; for example, demonstrating that print is read from left to right. Shared reading also enables the practitioner to draw attention to high frequency words, the spelling patterns of different words and punctuation. Where appropriate, the practitioner should cover words and ask the children to guess which word would make sense in the context. This could also link with phonic work where the children could predict the word based on seeing the initial phoneme. Multiple readings of the same text enable them to become familiar with story language and tune in to the way written language is organised into sentences.

Independent reading

As children become more confident with the written word they should be encouraged to recognise high frequency words. Practitioners should draw attention to these words during shared reading and shared writing. Children should have the opportunity to read these words in context and to play word matching and word recognition games. Encourage the children to use their ability to hear the sounds at various points in words and to use their knowledge of those phonemes to decode simple words.

Writing

Shared writing

Writing opportunities should include teacher demonstration, teacher scribing, copy writing and independent writing. (Suggestions for incorporating shared writing are given each week.)

Emergent writing

The role play area should provide ample opportunities for children to write purposefully, linking their writing with the task in hand. These meaningful writing opportunities help children to understand more about the writing process and to seek to communicate in writing. Children's emergent writing should occur alongside their increasing awareness of the 'correct' form of spellings. In the example below, the child is beginning to have an understanding of letter shapes as well as the need to write from left to right.

Assessment

When children are actively engaged in the role play area this offers ample opportunities for practitioners to undertake observational assessments. By participating in the role play area the practitioner can take time to talk in role to the children about their work and assess their performance. The assessment grid on page 40 enables practitioners to record progress through the appropriate Stepping Stone or Early Learning Goal.

DfES publications

The following publications will be useful:

Progression in Phonics (DfES 0178/2000)
Developing Early Writing (DfES 0055/2001)
Playing with Sounds (DfES 0280/2004)

Ourselves planning chart

Ourselves	Role play area	Personal, Social and Emotional Development	Communication, Language and Literacy	Knowledge and Understanding of the World	Mathematical Development	Creative Development	Physical Development
Week 1	Exploring the baby's nursery	Form good relations with peers Singing 'Welcome Song' Talking about families	Link sounds and letters Learning the alphabet Writing labels for nursery	Find out about everyday technology Looking at photographs of babies What would be a suitable toy for a baby?	Solve practical problems Finding out birthday dates Who is the tallest?	Use a range of tools Creating wallpaper for nursery Making furniture for nursery	Move with control and coordination Changing a nappy Bathing the baby Movements – how babies and toddlers move
Week 2	Making nursery mobiles and furniture	Understand different needs of people Modelling questions and answers Talking about families	Use phonics to write simple words Playing lullabies Sounding out cvc words Have writing table in nursery for emergent writing	Find out about past and present events in own lives Enacting scenarios around new babies Looking at family roles	Say and use number names Creating telephone numbers Counting different objects	Explore colour, shape, form and space Taking photographs Making silhouettes Making mobile for nursery	Move with confidence Performing actions to songs
Week 3	Discussing emotions and feelings	Expect others to treat their needs, views and beliefs with respect Asking questions Using puppets for role play	Use a pencil and hold it effectively Practising handwriting Encourage unaided writing Making a one-cut book about emotions	Ask questions Exploring feelings and emotions	Use maths to solve practical problems Making data collection and displaying as graph	Use imagination in role play Making masks Making biscuit faces Making finger puppets	Show awareness of space Parachute games
Week 4	Making a kitchen	Manage own personal hygiene Washing hands Favourite food	Attempt writing for different purposes Writing a food alphabet Writing instructions for making a jam sandwich	Investigate objects using all senses Talking about five senses Investigating sweet and savoury foods	Use language of 'more' and 'less' Counting objects in role play area Talking about shapes Comparing 'more' and 'less'	Explore colour, texture and shape Making a worktop and sink Making a cooker and dishwasher	Use range of large and small equipment Using utensils in sand and water play Holding a 'pancake race'
Week 5	Exploring senses of sight and hearing	Understand people have different needs Exploring senses of sight and hearing Discussing effect of loss of these senses	Listen carefully and speak clearly Sharing non-fiction book Playing a whispering game Following instructions Using sign language	Investigate objects using senses Discussing what we can see Experimenting with activities for sight and hearing	Use language to describe shape Looking for similar shapes in kitchen Sequencing shapes according to different criteria	Use imagination in art and design Painting face with eyes closed Creating a collage Making a telephone	Move with control and coordination Playing 'Hunt the wooden spoon', ball games, 'Sausages in the pan' and 'Fishes in the harbour'
Week 6	Exploring the senses in the kitchen	Expect others to treat their views with respect Discussing feelings and pain Safety in the home	Use a pencil and hold it effectively Writing labels Writing simple sentences	Investigate objects using senses Collecting equipment and discussing purposes Comparing different textures	Use ideas to solve practical problems Sorting and categorising kitchen equipment Making a bar graph Counting in 5s and 10s	Explore texture, shape and form Making a soft toy Holding a toys' party	Use range of large and small equipment Playing 'textures' game Gymnastics

Ourselves

In this six-week unit, the children will explore growth from birth to adulthood. They will have the opportunity to reflect on all kinds of families. They will discuss a range of emotions and feelings, and explore the five senses. The role play area will first become **a baby's nursery** and later in the unit it will become **the kitchen**.

In preparation for the unit, collect a range of baby items – for example, dolls, feeding bottles, baby blankets, shawls, baby clothes, nappies, baby bath, towels, sponge, pram, pushchair and highchair. For the kitchen role play, collect aprons, kitchen utensils, crockery, cutlery and a chef's hat. If possible, invite a mother and baby to visit the class over the course of the unit. Perhaps the children could observe the baby being fed, changed and bathed. At the end of the unit children will have learned about themselves, childcare and growing up. For Weeks 5 and 6, invite a sight-impaired person or a dog trainer for the blind to come in and talk to the children.

They will have made:
- wallpaper for the nursery
- baby toys
- worktop and sink
- soft toy
- changing table
- mobiles
- cooker and dishwasher
- collage
- cot
- masks and finger puppets
- Braille relief picture

WEEK 1

Starting the role play area

This week, the role play area will become a baby's nursery. The children will make a **frieze**, a **changing table** and a **cot**. During the week let the children go into the nursery and take on roles such as the mother, father and grandparent. They will learn about babies and growth and, through stories and rhymes, begin to find similarities and differences between humans. Adults should participate in the role play area by taking on a role such as a tired mum or a jealous sibling.

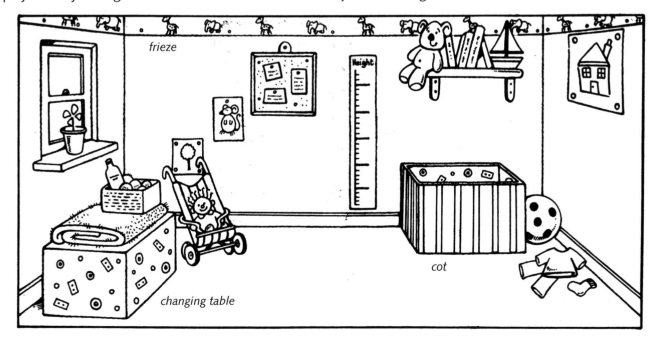

Week 1 – The nursery

Resources

Photocopiables:

Poems and songs 1 (page 33)
Making nursery furniture and toys (page 36)

Fiction books:

Babies by Ros Asquith and Sam Williams, Macmillan Children's Books (0 333963 94 6)
Brand New Baby by Bob Graham, Walker Books (0 744569 70 2)
Along Came Eric by Gus Clarke, Andersen Press (0 862648 56 4)
Here Come the Babies by Laurence and Catherine Anholt, Walker Books (0 744536 17 0)
Za-za's Baby Brother by Lucy Cousins, Walker Books (0 744547 64 4)
Sophie and the New Baby by Laurence Anholt, Orchard Books (1 841210 57 9)
Big Book of Families by Catherine and Laurence Anholt, Walker Books (0 744549 59 0)

Non-fiction books:

Myself Discovered Through Art and Technology by Karen Bryant-Mole, A&C Black (0 713643 73 0)
Babies Pack, Longman (0 582335 36 1)
Babies (Big Book) by Bobbie Neate, Longman (0 582339 55 3)
How Babies Grow (Big Book) by Bobbie Neate and Susan Henry, Longman (0 582339 54 5)
Ourselves: Babies by Henry Pluckrose, Franklin Watts (0 749651 96 2)
Ourselves: Babies 'Toppers' series by Nicola Baxter, Franklin Watts (0 749652 21 7)

Music and songs:

Bobby Shaftoe Clap Your Hands by Sue Nicholls, A&C Black (0 713635 56 8)
The Handy Band by Sue Nicholls, A&C Black (0 713668 97 0)

Materials:

- Large boxes
- Digital camera
- Photographs of children in the class as babies
- Two pieces of fabric in different colours, approx 60cm square
- Examples of nursery wallpaper
- Stencil or picture stamps
- 'Special box' (a box with a mirror in the base)
- White fabric for nappies

Software:

'Alphabet Soup' by 2Simple Software (www.2simple.com)

Personal, Social and Emotional Development

 Form good relationships with peers.

Introduce the topic 'Ourselves'. Tell the children that they are going to think and learn about themselves, their families and other people. They will learn about how and why everyone is special and how we are all different.

Circle time

❑ Sing a 'welcome song', such as 'The Welcome Song' from *Bobby Shaftoe Clap Your Hands* (see Resources) or make up your own – for example, to the tune of 'The Wheels on the Bus':

The children in our class have lots of names, lots of names, lots of names;
The children in our class have lots of names;
Here they are:
Connor and Joseph and Robert and Jack;
Catherine and Ruth and Parvindar and Tom;
Ahmed and Courtney and Mollie and Jade;
Here they are.

❑ Encourage the children to talk about themselves. Go round the circle asking each child to introduce himself or herself to the class. Give them a 'speaking frame' to support their introductions – for example, 'My name is …. I am … years old. I live with my … and my big sister ….'

❑ Go round the circle and talk about special attributes each child has. For example, 'Harry always has a big smile on his face so I'm calling him "Smiling Harry". Bethany is very good at drawing so I'll call her "Artistic Bethany".'

❑ Pass round the 'Special box' (see Resources). Tell the children to look inside the box and see who is special. They must keep very quiet and not say who the special person is. When everybody has had a turn ask them who is special – 'Me!'

New babies

❑ Ask the class if they know anyone who has had a new baby. Encourage discussion about babies. Who looks after the baby? Talk about how small babies are when they are born, feeding, learning to crawl,

Week 1 – The nursery

learning to walk and learning to talk. Why do babies cry? Let them role play holding a new baby.
- Share with the children a suitable non-fiction text about babies (see Resources).
- Talk about all the things a baby needs in the nursery.

Mathematical Development

 Use developing mathematical ideas and methods to solve practical problems.

Comparisons and sorting

- Ask the children to sit in a circle. Place two pieces of fabric of different colours (for example, red and white) in the centre of the circle. Choose six children to stand up (some boys and some girls). Ask the rest: How many children are standing up? Are they all boys? Are they all girls? Tell the children you are going to sort the group of children into two groups. Ask the boys to go and stand on the red fabric and ask the girls to stand on the white fabric. Count each group and ask the other children to say which is the larger or smaller group.
- Repeat this using different criteria such as hair colour, eye colour, wearing socks or wearing tights.
- Select three children to stand facing the class. Ask the class: Who is the tallest? Who is the shortest? Can you put these children in order of height, starting with the tallest? When the concept has been understood, increase the number of children at the front.

Dates and birthdays

- Talk to the children about their special day – their birthday. Chant the months of the year.
- Find out the date of each child's birthday. Make a simple block graph to show birthdays in the class. Write the months of the year along the bottom of a large sheet of card. Instruct each child to write his or her name on a square of paper. Stick the squares above the appropriate month in the correct order.

Extension

- Ask questions such as: Which month has the most birthdays? Are there more birthdays in November or December? Demonstrate writing the date for each child. Ask the children to practise writing their birth date on a whiteboard, concentrating on number formation.

Communication, Language and Literacy

 Link sounds and letters, naming and sounding the letters of the alphabet.

Listening and talking

- Read a story from the fiction list or a similar book. Discuss the story and ask the children what they liked about it.
- Learn a poem from those on page 33 about babies. Ask the children if they agree with the poem about the things that babies do.
- Look at the photographs of the children as babies and talk about anything they may remember. Ask them to write their full name on a piece of paper or card to label their photographs (See Knowledge and Understanding of the World).

Learning the alphabet

- Sing the alphabet to the tune of 'Auld Lang Syne'. Point out to the children that these are letter names.
- Make an alphabet of children's first names. On a large sheet of paper or on a whiteboard, write the letters of the alphabet in a vertical list. Remind the children about their discussion during circle time: 'We are all special.' Tell them that they were given their special names by their parents. Ask the children to help you to say the names of all the children in the class. Write the names in alphabetical order. Point out that we always use a capital letter at the beginning of names. If there are no children in the class with names starting with some letters, ask the children for suggestions of a name for that letter. Explain that there are very few names beginning with Q and X so we could use the names Quentin and Xanthe.

Starting with role play – Ourselves

Week 1 – The nursery

- Explain to the children that they are going to make an alphabet frieze with a picture of a child for each letter of the alphabet. Give each child an A4 piece of paper folded in half. On the inside, above the fold, write a child's name in yellow highlighter pen. Below the fold, draw an oval face shape. On the outside of the paper write the capital letter for the name in block lettering. Ask the children to add facial features to their face oval – eyes, nose, mouth, hair and so on. When the faces have been drawn, ask them to go over the highlighted name using a pencil. Then ask them to colour in the block letter on the outside of the page. Tell them to refer to the alphabet chart and to help you to display the pictures of the lift-the-flap children's faces in alphabetical order around the classroom.

Shared writing

- Model writing labels for pots of cream, talcum powder, baby wipes, nappies, shampoo, oil and so on. Discuss the formation of each letter and emphasise initial phonemes. Ask the children: What sound do you think comes next? Ask them where the labels should be placed in the role play area (on the wall or on a table). Encourage them to place the objects near to the appropriate labels.
- Demonstrate writing labels for the chairs and tables. Challenge the children to stick the labels on the correct objects.

Extension

- Ask individual children to draw pictures of things in the nursery and to add their own labels.

ICT

- If possible, let the children use 'Alphabet Soup' or other appropriate software.

Knowledge and Understanding of the World

 Find out about and identify the use of everyday technology.

Photography

At the beginning of the week, ask the children to bring in a photograph of themselves as babies.

- In small groups, talk about the photographs. Ask questions such as: How old were you then? How old are you now? How have you changed? What can you do now that you couldn't do then?
- Show the children how to take a photograph with a digital camera. With adult supervision, ask them to take a photograph of another child. Print these pictures and display, if possible in the nursery, alongside the baby photographs.

Talking about babies

- In the role play area, sit with groups of children to consider babies' needs. Ask questions such as: Who looks after babies? What do they eat? What do they wear? Why do we have to be careful and gentle with them? What else do they need? (Plenty of sleep)
- Help the children to think about suitable toys for a baby. Encourage them to consider materials, safety, colours and texture. Consider what toys could be put in the baby's room – for example, rattles, soft toys and mobiles.

Week 1 – The nursery

Creative Development

 Express and communicate ideas by using a range of tools and materials.

Making a nursery

❑ Tell the children they are going to create a wallpaper frieze for the nursery. Show them some examples of nursery wallpaper. Provide large sheets of paper, pencils, crayons and felt-tipped pens. Ask them to choose a stencil or a picture stamp to create a pattern for the wallpaper. Display the frieze in the nursery.

❑ Show the children pictures of nursery furniture (for example, from a catalogue) and discuss their purpose. Explain that they are going to make a changing table, a cot and some rattles for the nursery (see page 36).

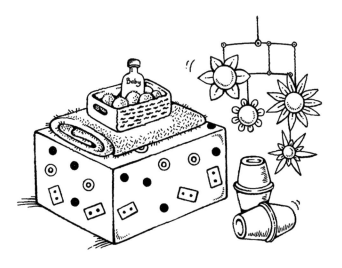

Physical Development

 Move with control and coordination.

Changing a nappy

❑ Show the children how to change a nappy. Ask them to do the same for the 'babies' in the nursery. Safety: Say they should never try this with a real baby.

Bathing a baby

❑ Fill the water tray with warm water and baby bubble bath. Ask questions such as: What do the bubbles feel like? How can you make more bubbles? What do the bubbles smell like? When you have a bath, do you have warm or cold water? Why?

❑ When everyone has had the opportunity to experiment with the bubbles, introduce two washable dolls and sponges. Allow the children to bath the dolls. As they play, encourage them to be gentle, use the sponges carefully and keep the water in the tray!

Movement

❑ Ask the children to think about how babies and toddlers move. Ask them to rock from side to side; lie on their tummy and push themselves up with their arms; crawl on hands and knees. Ask the children to stand up and pretend to walk unsteadily, then walk, run and skip. Talk about the sequence of movements. For example, first a baby lies in its cot, then it sits up and then it crawls. Later on it stands, walks and runs.

Starting with role play – Ourselves

Ourselves

WEEK 2

The role play area

This week, the baby's room will be used to explore the theme 'Me, my family and friends'. The children will be encouraged to use their knowledge from previous experiences in their role play. They will role play using the telephone and bringing a new baby home. They will complete the nursery by making **mobiles** and creating **self-portraits** and **silhouettes** to display on the walls.

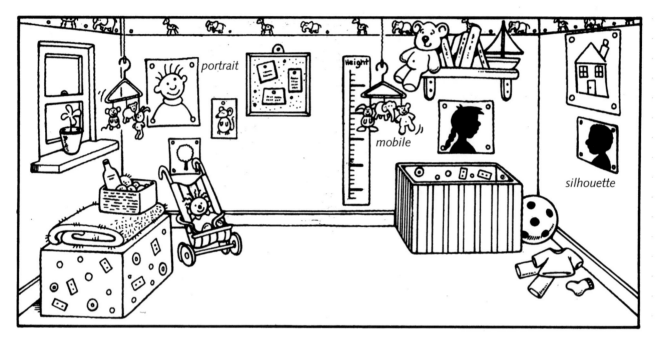

Resources

Photocopiables:

Poems and songs 1 (pages 33)

Fiction books:

I'm a Big Brother by Joanna Cole, William Morrow (0 688145 07 8)
Friends by Kim Lewis, Walker Books (0 744563 38 0)
Full, full, full of Love by Trish Cooke, Walker Books (1 844287 82 3)
You'll soon grow into them, Titch by Pat Hutchings, Red Fox (0 099207 11 7)
When Grandma Came by Jill Paton Walsh, Puffin (0 140543 27 9)

Non-fiction books:

Science Directions: Early Years Big Book, Collins (0 003172 41 4)
Being kind, 'Growing Up' series, Evans (1 842340 05 0)
Ourselves: Growing up by Henry Pluckrose, Franklin Watts (0 749651 96 2)

Music and songs:

Warm Up Time With the Sticky Kids, Action song: 'I get out of bed in the morning and hope it's a very nice day' (Audio cassette 1 857811 24 0)
The Handy Band by Sue Nicholls, A&C Black (0 713668 97 0)
Bobby Shaftoe Clap Your Hands, 'Hand upon your head' by Sue Nicholls, A&C Black (0 713635 56 8)
Tom Thumb's Musical Maths by Helen MacGregor, A&C Black (0 713649 71 2)
Tape or CD nursery rhymes
Lullaby music, such as Brahms
Everything's Growing by Niki Davies, Warner Chappell Publications, International Music Publications (1 859096 07 7)
Bingo Lingo by Helen MacGregor, A&C Black (0 713650 75 3)

Materials:

- Hoops or wire coat hangers
- String or thread
- Telephone
- Writing table and stationery
- Small boxes, lids, pipe cleaners, scraps of fabric, tissue and crepe paper
- Torch or lamp
- Phoneme cards or petals (a,b,c,d,e,g) x 2
- White chalk

Software:

All About Me CD-Rom, Dorling Kindersley (exploring family and friends) (0 751317 69 1)

Week 2 – Me, my family and friends

Personal, Social and Emotional Development

 Understand that people have different needs and should be treated with respect.

Hot seating

- Invite the children to ask you questions about your family. Try to ensure they ask you about your parents, brothers, sisters and so on. Model how to ask and answer the questions. Invite individual children to take over the hot seat and to talk about the members of their family. Role play being different members of a family.

Partner talk

- Ask the children to find a partner and sit in a space facing one another. Tell them that they are going to talk about their family with their partner. Remind them of the questions they asked you.

Mathematical Development

 Say and use number names in order and in familiar contexts.

Telephone numbers

- Ask the children if they can remember their telephone number. Talk about other telephone numbers they might need to know. Talk about where we can find telephone numbers. Role play using the telephone.

Extension

- Make a simple telephone directory for the role play area. On card, ask the children to draw pictures of different people – for example, grandparents, aunts and uncles, doctor or school friend. By each drawing, add a seven-figure number – for example, 4598311. Place this directory in the role play area.

Counting

- Encourage the children to count in the role play area. For example: How many babies are there in the nursery? If one goes out in the pram, how many babies are left? How many legs can you count on the babies? How many arms? How many nappies will you need for all the babies?
- Number the cots in the role play area. Help the children to write the numbers on card to display above the cots. Use these numbers to identify the cots – for example, 'Can you fetch me the baby in number 3 cot?'
- Sing 'Babies in their cots' from *Tom Thumb's Musical Maths* (see Resources).

Communication, Language and Literacy

 Use phonic knowledge to write simple, regular words.

Listening

- Read a story from the fiction list or a similar story. Discuss the themes and issues.
- Share a non-fiction book linked to the topic (see Resources). Talk about new ideas and concepts. Leave the book for the children to read or browse through.
- Read and discuss one of the poems about babies from page 33.

Shared reading

- Show the children a picture of a busy family. Encourage them to tell a story from the picture. Ask questions such as: What do you think they are doing? What do other people in your family like to do?

Emergent writing

- Introduce a writing table into the role play area. Provide a selection of writing tools and paper. Model writing lists of jobs to do – for example, give baby a bottle, bath baby, feed baby, put baby in the cot to sleep.

Starting *with role play – Ourselves*

Week 2 – Me, my family and friends

Lullabies

- Play lullabies such as Brahms' 'Lullaby'. Ask the children how the music made them feel and talk about lullabies. Ask questions such as: Why do people sing lullabies to their babies? Do they sing quietly or loudly, and why?
- Sing 'Bye Baby Bunting' or 'Rock-a-bye baby on the tree top'. Experiment, singing the rhyme loudly and quietly. Which would be best for baby?
- Sing 'Baby's bed' from *Bingo Lingo (See Resources)*. Talk about the spelling of each cvc word (consonant–vowel–consonant), such as 'cot'.

Phonics

- Ask the children how many letter sounds they can hear in the word 'bed'. Sound them out and ask them to count. Were they right? Write the word 'bed' on the board, sounding out the letters as you write. Write the letter 'r' on the board and ask the children what sound it makes. Show them how you can write 'red' and point out the similarities with 'bed'. Continue with 'fed', 'led', 'ted' and 'wed'.

Extension

- Show the children how you can change the end consonant to make new words. Ask them how many sounds there are in 'bag'. Write the word on the board. Ask them what word you make if you take off the last letter and add 't' (bat). Continue with 'bad', 'ban' and 'back'.
- Ask the children to write the letters 'bi' on their whiteboards. Say some letter sounds and ask them to write the word – for example, 'bit', 'big', 'bin', 'bib' and 'bid'.

Knowledge and Understanding of the World

 Find out about past and present events in their own lives, and in those of their families.

The new baby

- Throughout the week, take small groups of children into the role play area and create a scenario – for example, Mummy is bringing the new baby home from the hospital. Daddy will be with her. Everyone is very excited. Grandma and Grandad have been invited too. Help the children to discuss the scenario and negotiate roles. The teacher or other adult could take on one of the roles and take opportunities to model, question and develop the role play.
- Tell the children to telephone friends and family about the baby. Encourage them to refer to the 'telephone directory', saying the numbers as they dial. (See Mathematical Development.)

Family roles

- Discuss with the children each person's role within the family. Ask questions such as: Who does the cooking? Who does the gardening? Do you help Mummy in the kitchen? Who cleans the house?
- Sing 'Daddy's in the garden' from *Everything's Growing* (see Resources).

Week 2 – Me, my family and friends

Creative Development

 Explore colour, texture, shape, form and space in two or three dimensions.

Taking photographs

- Tell the class that you are going to be a photographer and take a family portrait. Take groups of children into the role play area and direct children to be different family members – for example, Grandad, Mum and little sister. Use hats as props. Arrange the 'family members' for the photograph. Using a digital camera, take the picture. Display the photographs in a small album.
- Ask the children to draw their family portrait. Encourage them to show differences in height and size. Ask them to think about the colours they use. Talk about how you can make someone look old.

Portraits

- Give each child an oval face shape template. Ask them to add features using paints. They could use wool for hair. Ask the children to think about skin, hair and eye colour.

Silhouettes

- You will need: a torch or lamp, black sugar paper (fixed to the wall or an easel) and white chalk. Tell a child to sit in profile in front of the paper. Shine the lamp to create a silhouette. Ask another child to draw around the silhouette with chalk. Cut them out and display them around the room. Encourage the children to guess who is who from the silhouettes.

Mobiles

- Ask the children to think of ideas for mobiles to suspend in the baby's room. Provide a selection of small boxes, lids, pipe cleaners, paints and scraps of fabric and paper. Ask them to choose a character for their mobile – for example, a rabbit, elephant or teddy bear. Talk about a suitable size and weight and hang these models from hoops or coat hangers. Suspend from the ceiling above the cot. Talk about the mobiles. Will they attract the baby's attention? Why?

ICT

- 'All About Me' CD-Rom, Dorling Kindersley – exploring family and friends.

Physical Development

 Move with confidence, imagination and in safety.

Music and movement

- Make up a movement song with the children. Sing and move to the traditional tune of 'This is the way the farmer rides'. Sing:

    This is the way my baby crawls ... wriggle, crawl, wriggle, crawl, wriggle, crawl.
    This is the way my mummy moves ... busy, busy.
    This is the way my daddy walks ... big strides, big strides.
    This is the way my grandad walks ... creak, groan, creak, groan.

- Do the actions to one or both of the following songs: 'Grandad's Whiskers' or 'I get out of bed in the morning' from *Everything's Growing* (See Resources).

Ourselves

WEEK 3

The role play area

This week the role play area will be used by the children to explore emotions and feelings. The children will create **masks** to show expressions and **finger puppets** for drama. They will also draw up simple databases with information related to themselves.

Resources

Photocopiables:

Poems and songs 2 (page 34)
Handwriting patterns (page 37)

Fiction books:

The Lion Who Wanted To Love by Giles Andreae, Orchard Books (1 860399 13 4)
The Huge Bag of Worries by Virginia Ironside, Hodder Wayland (0 750021 24 1)
If you're happy and you know it by Jan Ormerod and Lindsey Gardiner, OUP (0 192725 51 3)
Susan Laughs by Jeanne Willis and Tony Ross, Red Fox (0 099407 56 6)
The bad tempered ladybird by Eric Carle, Puffin (0 140503 98 6)
Temper Temper by Norman Silver, Hodder Wayland (0 750027 04 5)

Non-fiction books:

I feel sad by Mike Gordon, 'Your emotions' series, Hodder Wayland (0 750214 06 6)
What Makes Me Happy? by Catherine and Laurence Anholt, Walker Books (0 744560 69 1)
Our World – Our Feelings From Happy to Sad, 'Little Nippers' series, Heinemann Library (0 431162 52 2)

Poetry:

Mud Between the Toes, Wendy Cooling (ed), Franklin Watts (0 749650 07 9)

Music and songs:

The Handy Band by Sue Nicholls, A&C Black (0 713668 97 0)
Alleluya! 77 Songs for Thinking People, A&C Black (0 713619 98 8)
Bingo Lingo by Helen Macgregor, A&C Black (0 713650 75 3)

Materials:

- Two hand puppets
- Safety mirrors
- Card and sticks
- Wool for hair
- Parachute (LDA LL07097)
- A tube made out of rolled card to fit the child's index finger and two circles of card for the face
- Card face template for children to draw round
- Cards or posters showing emotions, such as Emotions (LDA LL06006)
- Plain biscuits, such as digestive or Rich Tea
- Coloured writing icing

Week 3 – Emotions and feelings

Personal, Social and Emotional Development

 Understand that they can expect others to treat their needs, views and beliefs with respect.

Circle time

- Encourage the children to consider what happens 'if'. Ask questions such as: If you say something unkind to your friends, how will they feel? If you help Mummy to carry the shopping, how will she feel? If you are unkind to your baby brother, how do you feel?
- Using the two hand puppets, pretend that they have had a quarrel. One of the puppets has called the other a nasty name and the other puppet is crying. Ask the children what they should do to become friends again. Talk about saying sorry.
- In the kitchen area set up a kindness chart. Every time anyone is very kind add this to the chart.

> Joseph was kind when he helped Anil.
>
> Bethany was kind when she gave her toy to Peter.

- Ask the children to sit in a circle. Each child should take it in turns to face the child on their left and say 'Hello, hello. How do you do? Shake hands to say, how are you?' Pass the handshake round the circle.
- Sing 'Love is something if you give it away' from *Alleluya!* and talk about caring for others.

Mathematical Development

 Use developing mathematical ideas and methods to solve practical problems.

Simple data collection and block graphs

- On a large sheet of paper, draw the frame for a block graph to show different hair colours. Divide the bottom line of the graph into four sections, for blonde hair, brown hair, black hair and red hair.
- Give each child a square of paper and ask them to draw a picture of themselves showing their hair colour. Ask them to write their name on their picture. The children then stick their picture above the appropriate colour.
- Ask questions about the data, such as: How many children have blonde hair? Are there more children with brown hair than black?

Extension

- Invite more able children to draw a graph to show, for example, favourite games, pets or toys.

Communication, Language and Literacy

 Use a pencil and hold it effectively to form recognisable letters, most of which are correctly formed.

Listening

- Read the class a story from the fiction book list. Talk about the feelings of the characters.
- Read the poem 'What are friends like?' (page 34) and talk about friendship.

Handwriting

- Talk about forming letters. Choose one of the handwriting patterns – for example, 'c', 'u' or 'm' and encourage the children to draw the letters in the air with you. Give each child a copy of page 37 to practise handwriting patterns.

Starting with role play – Autumn Book 1

Week 3 – Emotions and feelings

Shared writing

- Explain to the class that they are going to make a class book about different feelings. Show them pictures of people showing different emotions. Write the different emotions on the board – for example, happy, sad, angry and excited. Take one of the pictures and ask the children what the person might be feeling (for example, sad). Ask what makes them sad. Model writing: 'I feel sad when …' Talk about letter formation and orientation. Repeat this with other emotions.

- Make a book for each child out of paper. Write in highlighter at the top of each page, 'I am happy when…' and ask the children to draw one thing on each page that makes them feel happy.

Extension

- Invite more able children to write 'I feel happy when…' for each of their pictures. Remind them about correct letter formation.

Unaided writing

- In the role play area, place a box, some sheets of paper and writing tools. Explain that it is a 'feelings' box. Invite the children to write down their thoughts, such as 'I am feeling lonely because my best friend is away today.' Encourage the children to try this writing for themselves. Share some of the thoughts together during circle time.

Singing

- Sing 'When I feel sad' from *Bingo Lingo* (See Resources).

Knowledge and Understanding of the World

 Ask questions about why things happen.

Feelings

- Explore feelings and emotions with the group. Direct the children to consider why babies cry. What do parents do to stop the baby crying? What makes a baby laugh? What would they do to make a baby laugh? In the role play area, set up a scenario in which Daddy is watching football on television and the baby is crying. What will he do? Set up another in which the baby is ill and the parents are worried. How do they feel? What will they do?

Making masks

Creative Development

 Use their imagination in …. imaginative and role play.

- Give each child a card face template showing eyes and nose. Ask them to draw around the template onto card and cut it out. Help them to cut holes for eyes. Ask them to choose an emotion or feeling. Encourage them to show that emotion through facial expression. Look in the mirror. Ask them: Do you look surprised? How can you tell? What does your mouth do? Ask them to look at your eyebrows. Do they go up or down? Do you look happy? Does your mouth go up or down? Ask the children to add the facial features according to their chosen expression. Decorate with wool for hair. Attach the masks to sticks. Store the masks by sticking them to the wall using sticky tack to keep them readily available in the role play area. In the role play area, encourage the children to use their masks. They should explain the expression on their mask face and decide what has made them feel this way.

Hot seating

- Invite a child wearing his or her mask to sit in the hot seat. Support the rest of the class as they ask questions such as: Why are you so sad? What made you so happy? Why are you so surprised?

- After exploring these ideas, give the children time to

Week 3 – Emotions and feelings

play with the masks and make up their own role play of mini dramas or scenarios.

Biscuit faces

❏ Give each child a biscuit and ask them to create a face with the writing icing. Encourage them to create a face with an 'expression'. They could share their biscuits in school or take them home for their family.

Finger puppets

❏ Help the children to make a happy/sad finger puppet. Make a tube out of rolled card to fit the child's index finger. (Alternatively they could make a sock puppet.) Cut out two discs of card for the faces. Ask the children to colour a happy face on one circle of card and a sad face on the other and to add wool for hair. Glue the circles onto the front and back of the puppets. Let the children paint their finger puppets and add a paper collar or scarf if they wish. Show them how to role play scenes using the finger puppets, showing the happy face when things are going well and the sad face when they are not.

Physical Development

 Show awareness of space, of themselves and of others.

Fine motor skills

❏ Cutting out and drawing round templates (see Creative Development).

Parachute games

❏ Ask the children to stand around the parachute. Explain that they are going to see what happens when the parachute is lifted. Everyone holds the edge on the ground. Count one, two, three, UP! The children lift the parachute as high as they can and watch it inflate and float. Repeat this activity several times. Now explain that they are going to be given instructions to follow. When the parachute is next inflated, call out a sound such as 'a'. Those children whose names begin with 'a' let go of the parachute and run underneath to change places and catch it. Variations: those with blonde hair, those with blue eyes, those who are happy today. NB: establish rules about safety first – for example, look where you are going; you must not touch anyone as you travel under the parachute; you must stand still when you catch the parachute.

Ourselves

WEEK 4

The role play area

During this week, the role play area will be converted into a kitchen. The children will help to make a collection of kitchen utensils and will make a **worktop** and **sink**, a **cooker** and **dishwasher**. The children will also learn about two of the five senses – taste and smell. They will explore these, through their role play, scientific experiments and investigations related to taste and smell. (Be aware that some children may have food allergies.)

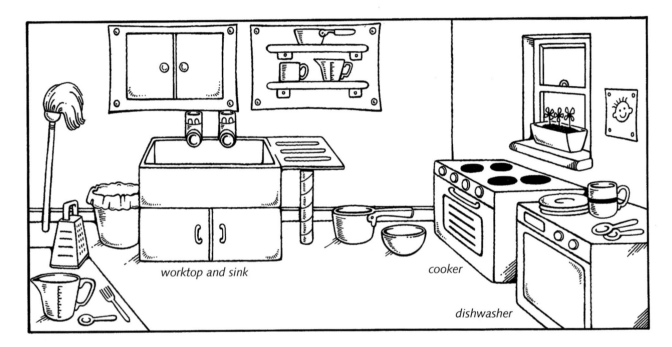

worktop and sink *cooker* *dishwasher*

Resources

Photocopiables:

Poems and songs 2 (page 34)
A jam sandwich (page 38)

Fiction books:

Mo's Smelly Jumper by David Bedford, Little Tiger Press (1 854309 10 2)
Oliver's Vegetables by Vivian French, Hodder Children's Books (0 340634 79 0)
Oliver's Milkshake by Vivian French, Hodder Children's Books (0 340754 54 0)
The Smelly Book by Babette Cole, Red Fox (0 099409 61 5)

Non-fiction books:

Sniffing and Smelling by Henry Pluckrose, Franklin Watts (0 749637 89 7)
Eating and Tasting by Henry Pluckrose, Franklin Watts (0 749637 90 0)
The Senses: Smell, Hodder Wayland (0 750214 09 0)
The Senses: Taste, Hodder Wayland (0 750214 10 4)

Materials:

- Kitchen utensils
- Aprons
- Chef's hats, if available
- Bowls, saucepans and frying pans
- Plates
- Spoons
- Collage materials
- Large boxes and cardboard tubes
- Oven trays (could be tinfoil trays)
- Perfume
- Bubble bath
- Peppermint essence
- Lemon juice
- Fabric conditioner
- Selection of toy foods
- Pictures of different foods
- Paper plates
- Selection of sweet and savoury foods (small amounts)
- Juices – for example, orange, lemon, blackcurrant
- Sliced bread, margarine spread and jam
- Crisps – for example, plain, cheese and onion, prawn cocktail

Week 4 – Taste and smell in the kitchen

Personal, Social and Emotional Development

 Manage their own personal hygiene.

Personal hygiene

- Encourage the children to think and talk about the importance of washing their hands before coming into contact with food. Explain that it is their responsibility to do this independently.

Group discussion

- Talk about favourite foods and meals. Ask questions such as: Why do you like that? What does it taste like? Why don't you like that? Encourage the children to listen to the views of others and to add their own comments and ideas.

Knowledge and Understanding of the World

 Investigate objects and materials by using all of their senses as appropriate.

The senses

- Talk about the five senses with the children. Tell them that their brain is like a control centre for the body and that messages are sent to it by nerves, which are rather like long wires throughout the body that are attached to the brain. Discuss the following questions: How do you know if it is day or night? (Sight) How do you know if someone is speaking to you? (Hearing) How do you know if you like to eat something? (Taste) How do you know something is cooking? (Smell) How do you know that something is hard or soft? (Touch) Tell the children about the sense organs and identify them.
- Tell the children that we use our noses to smell things. In water trays, add perfumed bubble bath, peppermint essence, lemon juice and fabric conditioner. Encourage the children to talk about the smells. Ask questions such as: Do you like them? Why? What smells do you like? What smells don't you like? (Be aware of allergies.)

Investigations

Sweet or savoury

- Prepare a selection of sweet and savoury foods – for example, jam, sugar, honey, cheese, cold meat, Marmite, apple, plain crisps – each one in a paper baking case. Have two sheets of paper labelled 'sweet' and 'savoury'. Offer the children a selection of the sweet and savoury foods listed above. Ask them to taste tiny portions. Ask if it is sweet or savoury. How do they know? Which of their senses are they using? Record findings by writing the food on the appropriate sheet of paper.

Linking smell to taste

- Place a small amount of different flavoured fresh fruit juices in small plastic containers. Show the children the containers and tell them which flavour is in each. Give them a small amount to taste. Ask: How do you know which is which? Can you tell me what flavour juice you are drinking? Now ask the children to try this with their eyes shut (they may use a blindfold), then with their eyes shut and holding their nose. Ask: Can you tell which flavour is which? Why was it more difficult?
- Put three flavours of crisps in separate bowls. Ask the children to taste and identify them. (A sip of water between each may help.) Then ask them to close their eyes while you switch the bowls around. Ask them to identify the flavours by smell. Ask: 'Which sense organ are you using for this?' Tell them to try again with their eyes closed and holding their nose. 'Is it easier or more difficult?' Tell them to try again with just their eyes closed and use their senses of smell and taste. Ask: 'Is this easier?'

Identifying sweet, sour and bitter

- Encourage the children to taste some sweet items – for example, apple or strawberry – and then some

Week 4 – Taste and smell in the kitchen

sour food – for example, lemon or unsweetened grapefruit. Encourage them to talk about their findings. Help them to use the appropriate vocabulary, such as tongue, taste buds, sweet, sour, bitter, savoury, smell, nose and swallow. Ask them what it would be like if they didn't have a sense of smell or taste. Link this to safety issues – for example, burning, gas, rotting food or milk that is off. Talk about being a scientist, trying to find out about things by testing and experimenting.

Mathematical Development

 Use language such as 'more' or 'less' to compare two numbers.

Counting

- Ask the children to find things in the role play area – for example, four spoons. Encourage them to count carefully and increase the challenge for the more able children.
- Talk about the different shapes you can see in the kitchen. What shape is the cooker? What shape is the table? Encourage the children to use the vocabulary of shape – for example, square, oblong, rectangle and circular.

More or less?

- Ask the children to work in pairs or small groups and to look at the pictures of food and decide which they like to eat. Make three cards labelled 'Yum', 'Yuk' and 'Maybe'. Tell the children to divide the food into three categories – 1. Yum (we all like); 2. Yuk (none of us likes); 3. Maybe (some like/some don't). Discuss which category has the most or least items of food – for example, are there more things children like than they dislike?

Extension

- Show the children some different sized packets of identical food and ask them to estimate which have more contents and which less. Show them how to read the weight of the contents to check their predictions.

Creative Development

 Explore colour, texture, shape, form and space in two or three dimensions.

Making a worktop and sink, cooker/dishwasher

- Either convert the changing table in the baby's room or cover and paint another box. Add taps, using cardboard tubes and other round objects or paint them on. Cover another box to create a worktop or place a table in the kitchen.
- Similarly, make a cooker and/or a dishwasher.

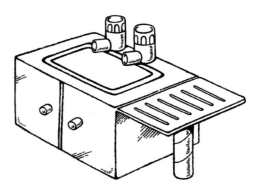

Extension

- Ask the children how they could make an oven with a door that opens and closes. (Velcro fastening.)

Create the background for the kitchen

- Paint large sheets of paper as open cupboards with shelves. Provide old catalogues and magazines with pictures of food products and kitchen equipment and gadgets. Ask the children to cut out pictures to stick on the shelves. Encourage them to be organised – for example, gadgets on one shelf, food on another. Display these collage pictures in the role play area.

Create an ideal meal

- Give each child a paper plate and different colours of play dough. Tell them to create their favourite meal.

Week 4 – Taste and smell in the kitchen

Communication, Language and Literacy

 Attempt writing for different purposes.

Speaking and listening

- Discuss the five senses and the sense organs. Share a non-fiction book from the Resources list or any other suitable title.
- Read the poem 'Today for lunch' (page 34) and discuss how the author makes the food sound good to eat.

Shared writing

- Find or draw pictures of the sense organs (ear, nose, mouth, eye, hand). Give them out to the group. Write the five senses on label cards: sight, hearing, smell, touch and taste. Discuss the letter formation and spelling as you write. Challenge children to come out with their picture of a sense organ and to position it under the correct sense.

Shared and independent writing

- Explain to the children that they are going to help you to write a food alphabet. Go through each letter of the alphabet and discuss items of food that start with that letter. (NB. some letters are difficult – for example, u = Ugli fruit; q = quiche; v = vinegar; x, y and z could be on the final page and represented by yogurt.) Give each child an A4 sheet of paper and a different letter of the alphabet. Tell them to draw a food item that starts with that letter. They should add a label for their picture.

Instructions – making a jam sandwich

- Ask the children if they have seen a cookery programme on television. Tell them they are going to make a jam sandwich, but first they need to list the ingredients and then explain the method. Write the ingredients on a board (sliced bread, margarine and jam). Ask the children to tell you how to make the jam sandwich. Demonstrate how to make it. Then ask each child to make their own jam sandwich.

Extension

- Make copies of page 38 and cut out the pictures. Give each child a set of the pictures to put in the correct sequence.

Physical Development

 Use a range of small and large equipment.

Cutting skills

See Creative Development.

Motor skills

- In the sand and water trays, provide a selection of kitchen utensils, such as spoons, scoops, sieves, funnels, jugs, pots and cups. Allow the children to play freely and to experiment with pouring, scooping, stirring, filling and emptying.

Music and song

- Sing 'This is the way we wash our hands/spread the jam/cut the bread/eat a sandwich' to the tune of 'Here we go round the mulberry bush'.

Outside play

Pancake races

- Make pancakes from circles of thick card that fit inside frying pans and saucepans. Show the children how to toss the pancakes. Who can toss one and catch it in the pan? Set them off on a race. When you call 'Stop!' they must stop running and toss their pancakes. Then they must run to the finish line.

Ourselves

WEEK 5

The role play area

During this week, the role play area, the kitchen, will be used by the children to investigate two more senses – sight and hearing. They will be presented with opportunities to do this through play, games and physical activity. They will talk about what it is like when you cannot see. They will make **telephones** and a **collage**.

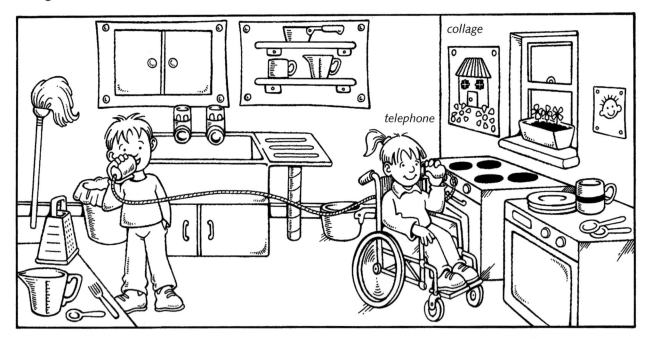

Resources

Photocopiables:

Poems and songs 3 (page 35)
Sign language signs (page 39)

Fiction books:

Private and Confidential by Marian Ripley, Frances Lincoln (0 711221 66 9)
The Happy Hedgehog Band by Martin Waddell, Walker Books (0 744530 49 0)

Non-fiction books:

Senses: Looking and Hearing by Henry Pluckrose, Franklin Watts (0 749637 87 0)
Looking and Seeing by Henry Pluckrose, Franklin Watts (0 749637 86 2)
The Senses: Sight, Hodder Wayland (0 750214 08 2)
The Senses: Hearing, Hodder Wayland (0 750214 07 4)
Friends: Going swimming – Rowan is deaf by Dianne Church, Franklin Watts (0 749638 01 X)
Friends: Going on a school trip – Georgia is blind by Dianne Church, Franklin Watts (0 749636 70 X)

Music and songs:

Come and Praise (He gave me eyes), BBC School Radio Publication
Alleluya! 77 Songs for Thinking People, A&C Black (0 713619 98 8)
Tom Thumb's Musical Maths by Helen MacGregor, A&C Black (0 713649 71 2)
Bobby Shaftoe Clap Your Hands by Sue Nicholls, A&C Black (0 713635 56 8)
Harlequin: 44 Songs Round the Year, A&C Black (0 713621 55 9)

Materials:

- Strands of coloured wool
- A five-minute sand timer
- Examples of Braille writing
- Paints and paper
- Collage materials including, for example, pieces of corrugated card
- Large balls
- Magnifying glasses and items to investigate (see page 25)
- Digital microscope
- Plastic cups
- 10m of thin string

Week 5 – Sight and sounds in the kitchen

Knowledge and Understanding of the World

 Investigate objects and materials by using all of their senses as appropriate.

Investigating sight

- Discuss with the children the things that they can see with their eyes – the blue sky, their family, a friend or a beautiful tree. Consider what might happen if we could not see: bumping into things; having accidents; difficulty finding one's way; difficulty reading books, and so on. Explain that some people need to wear glasses to help them see things better. Introduce the concept of short sight and long sight.
- Provide some magnifying glasses for the children to investigate objects and patterns in the kitchen. Also provide a selection of dishes containing, for example, salt, sugar, coffee granules, flour, sand, tea leaves, a tea bag and/or small pasta shapes. Give time for the children to investigate and talk about their findings. If possible, show them how to use a digital microscope and produce images on the computer.
- Ask the children how we can see things a very long way away, such as the Moon and stars. (Through a telescope)
- Draw a large, simple diagram of an eye and label the eyelashes, eyebrow, pupil, iris, eyelid, cornea (transparent covering of the eye) and tear duct.

Experiment

- Tell the children to hold a finger in front of them and bring it slowly towards their eyes. What happened? What did they feel? Tell the children to work in pairs and take it in turns to watch one another carefully and tell their partner what happened. Ask them to hold two fingers touching nail to nail in front of them, then bring them slowly towards their eyes. What did they see? (Three fingers)

Hearing

- Explain that the external part of the ear is shaped so that it catches sounds. Talk about how some animals, such as cats, can move their ears to improve their hearing.

Experiment

- Organise the children to work in pairs. Tell one child to drop a small object, such as a nail, onto the floor. Can the other child hear it? Then tell the child to try moving further away and then drop the object again. Can they still hear it? How far can they move away before the other child cannot hear the nail fall?

Listening game

- Play 'What's cooking?' Sit the children in a circle. Blindfold one child in the centre of the circle. Tell the children that when you touch one of them on the shoulder, they should say 'Mm, what's cooking today?'. Challenge the blindfolded child to point in the direction from which the sound came.
- Play 'Guess the object'. Show the children a small selection of kitchen implements, such as wooden and metal spoons, a saucepan, a Pyrex bowl, a plate and a tray. Demonstrate the sound made by tapping the wooden spoon against each object. Place a screen in front of the objects. Ask a child to go behind the screen and tap one of the objects. Who can guess which object was tapped? Can they find it and tap it too?

Environmental sounds

- Discuss loud and soft sounds in the environment.
- Sing 'The cook is in the kitchen' to the tune of 'The farmer's in his den'. (*The cook is in the kitchen. The cook is in the kitchen. Is he loud or is he quiet? The cook is in the kitchen.*) Invite the children to take turns to stand in the circle and tap with a spoon on different pieces of kitchen equipment loudly or quietly. Encourage the others to say whether the child in the centre of the ring is playing the 'drum' quietly or loudly.
- Put some dried peas or beans in plastic containers to make shakers. Play the same game as above, singing 'The cook is in the kitchen', using these shakers.

Week 5 – Sight and sounds in the kitchen

Personal, Social and Emotional Development

 Understand that people have different needs.

Circle time

- Read and discuss one of the suggested stories about being blind (see Resources).
- Consider what it must be like to be blind. In the role play kitchen encourage the children, in very small groups with adult support, to find objects with their eyes closed. Ask: How did you feel? How did you find your way around the kitchen? Do you know anyone who is blind?
- Talk about guide dogs for the blind and Braille writing. Discuss the dangers of not being able to see.
- Consider what it must be like to be deaf, to have no sense of hearing. Do the children know anyone who is deaf? Ask: How do you think deaf people communicate or 'talk' to each other? Introduce the idea of sign language.
- Ask the children to think of some of the sounds they would miss if they couldn't hear, such as friends talking, music playing and birds singing.

Using our senses

- Sing songs about seeing – for example, the hymn 'He gave me eyes so that I can see the wonders of the world'. (See Resources) Perform actions to this hymn as signs to others.
- Sing 'I can see cherries high up in a tree' from *44 Songs Round the Year*. (See Resources)
- Discuss with the children the dangers of not being able to hear – for example, a car coming when you are trying to cross the road.

Mathematical Development

 Use language such as 'circle' or 'bigger' to describe shape.

Shape

- Look at the plates, cans and other kitchen equipment. What shapes are they? Talk about the number of sides and corners. If possible, cut out pictures and ask the children to sort them. (Four sides, three sides and so on.)
- Encourage the children to use their sense of sight to look for similar shapes in the classroom and the local environment. Perhaps they could, in groups with an adult, go for a walk in the school grounds to look for shapes.
- Teach the children the following chant.

  I can see a circle here in our classroom.
  I can see a circle over there.
  If you can see a circle here in our classroom
  Please use your finger and show us where.

  First of all say the rhyme yourself and then encourage the children to take the lead. Do the same with other shapes.
- Sing 'Which shapes?' from *Tom Thumb's Musical Maths*. (See Resources)

Counting

- Sing 'Ten fat sausages sizzling in the pan' from *Tom Thumb's Musical Maths*. (See Resources)
- Read the poem 'Me and you' on page 34 and then ask the children to count the following on themselves: eyes, ears, nose, lips, elbows and chin.

Extension

- Add some of the body parts together – for example, hands and feet. Show the children how to represent this as a sum: 2 + 2 = 4.

Week 5 – Sight and sounds in the kitchen

Communication, Language and Literacy

 Listen carefully and speak clearly with confidence and control.

Listening

- Share with the children a non-fiction book (see Resources). Ask them what they have learned about blindness or deafness.
- Read and discuss one of the stories from the fiction list or another suitable book.
- Read the poem 'My eyes can see' on page 34 and invite the children to join in with the actions.
- Play the listening game 'Whispers'. In the kitchen, ask the children to sit in a circle. Start off a message to be whispered from one child to the next around the circle. For example, 'Suzie would like fish and chips for her tea tonight.' Challenge the children to really listen and pass the message accurately.
- Play a listening game. Sit the children either indoors in the kitchen or outdoors, and ask them to close their eyes for two minutes. Ask them to listen carefully for sounds they can hear. Then encourage them to recall and identify the sounds, sharing their ideas with others.

Singing

- Sing 'Listen, children' from *Bobby Shaftoe Clap Your Hands*. (See Resources)

Sign language

- Use a copy of page 39 to discuss sign language. Help the children to copy the signs and use them to communicate. Keep an enlarged copy for future reference.

Demonstration writing

- Link together some of the sign language actions to make a simple sentence; for example, 'I like you.' Go through the actions and then write the words for each action. (I like TV. Can you phone me?) Speak those words for which no signs are provided. Ask the children to read the sentences and copy the signs.

Creative Development

 Use their imagination in art and design.

Painting

- Challenge the children to paint a face with their eyes closed.

Making a collage

- Using collage materials, create a class textured picture that a blind person could feel – for example, of a house and garden or your kitchen. Encourage the children to concentrate on texture and relief – for example, a roof made of corrugated paper; flower petals from polystyrene chips. When the picture is finished, ask the children to close their eyes and run their fingers over the scene. Challenge them to identify each object just by touch.

Making a telephone

- You will need two plastic cups and 10m of thin string. Make a hole in the bottom of each cup and thread the string through. Tie a knot on the inside of each cup. Stretch the string tightly. Ask one child to talk into one cup and another child to listen with the other cup.

Week 5 – Sight and sounds in the kitchen

Physical Development

 Move with control and coordination.

The giant's treasure

- Ask the children to sit in a circle facing inwards, with one child (the giant) blindfolded in the middle. The giant is sleeping and guarding his treasure (a bunch of keys). One child in the circle tries to take his treasure. If the giant hears someone moving, he should point in the direction of the sound. If he is correct, then another child tries to steal the treasure.

Hunt the wooden spoon

- This game is based on 'Hunt the thimble'. One child goes out of the room or out of sight (with an adult) while another child hides a wooden spoon. As he searches, the class tell him whether he is getting closer or further away by calling 'warmer' or 'colder'.

Ball games

- Ask the children to find and sit facing a partner. Give each pair a large ball. Ask the children to gently roll the ball to each other. Allow them time to practise. Then ask them to try to repeat the activity with their eyes closed. Talk about their findings and select pairs to demonstrate.

Put the sausages in the pan

- In the kitchen, place a large, laminated picture of a frying pan on the wall. Blindfold a child and give him a small laminated picture of, for example, a string of sausages (with a ball of sticky tack on the back). Turn the child round once and ask him to 'Put the sausages in the pan.'

Outside play

Hunt the wool

- Hide strands of coloured wool at different heights in the outdoor play area. Show examples of the strands to the class and then ask them to go outside and find as many as they can in five minutes. (Show them the sand timer before they start.)

Fishes in the harbour

- Ask the children to sit in a circle facing inwards. Give each child the name of a fish, such as a shark, shrimp and swordfish. (It helps to touch each child on the head as you name them.) Check that everyone knows what fish they are. Call out, for example, 'All the sharks in the sea.' The sharks stand up and step back from the circle. They begin to run round the circle in the direction you indicate. Give instructions such as 'Tide turns,' (change direction); 'It's getting rougher,' (move faster); 'It's getting calmer,' (move more slowly); 'It's very choppy,' (hop). When you call out 'Sharks in the harbour!' the children must race back to their own place and sit down. Do the same with 'shrimps' and 'swordfish'. Occasionally call 'Fishes in the sea,' and **all** the children run round in a circle.

Ourselves

WEEK 6

The role play area

During this week, the children will use the role play area to explore the fifth of our senses – touch. They will make a variety of **play food**. They will learn that the sense of touch is in the skin and that messages are sent along the nerves to the brain. They will consider physical disability and its effects. At the end of the week, give time for reflection on what the children have learned about themselves, their feelings and emotions and their senses.

Draw the role play area to a close by holding a 'Ready, steady, cook' afternoon where children make a variety of play food to be served to guests. Bring in some children's recipe books and talk about the different ingredients.

Resources

Photocopiable:

Poems and songs 3 (page 35)

Fiction book:

Lucy's Picture by Nicola Moon, Orchard Books (1 852139 55 2)

Non-fiction books:

Senses: Touching and Feeling by Henry Pluckrose, Franklin Watts (0 749637 88 9)
Senses: Touch by Mandy Suhr, Hodder Wayland (0 750214 11 2)

Materials:

- Foods of different textures
- Bowls containing hot, warm and cold water
- Textured collage materials
- Fur fabric or felt templates of a cat or a teddy
- Needles and thread
- Some lengths of pipe cleaner for whiskers and a tail
- Some white and black felt rounds for eyes
- Old cut-up tights or fabric scraps for stuffing
- A piece of dowling or a wooden spoon to push the stuffing into the toy

Week 6 – Touch

Personal, Social and Emotional Development

 Understand that they can expect others to treat their views with respect.

Circle time

- Ask the children about the special toys they take to bed with them. Ask questions such as: Why do you like to cuddle them? What do the toys feel like? Who gives you cuddles? Why do you like to be cuddled? How do you feel when someone tickles you? What parts of your body are most ticklish? How do you feel when you fall over and graze your knee? How do you know when things are hot or cold to touch?
- Discuss safety in the home, particularly in the kitchen. If you touch something hot, nerve endings in your skin feel the pain and send a very quick message, like a telephone message, to your brain. This makes you stop and take your hand away as quickly as possible. We use our sense of touch to tell if the bath water is too hot or too cold. Have you ever touched something sharp? Have you ever cut yourself? How did it feel?
- Explain to the class that if you have no feeling in a part of your body, such as your legs, you cannot move – you are paralysed. Ask questions such as: How would you feel if you could not walk or could not feel your legs? When you feel pain or hurt yourself, do you like it? How do other people feel if we hurt them?

Knowledge and Understanding of the World

 Investigate objects and materials by using their senses as appropriate.

Investigations

- In the kitchen, make a collection of kitchen equipment of different textures. Ask the children why we have nothing made from glass. Ask them to hold each object in turn. Ask questions such as: What does it feel like? Is it hard or soft? Does it feel rough or smooth? Does it feel cold or warm?
- Compare metal and wooden objects. Which feels colder or warmer?
- Put an object into a bag. Ask a child to put his hand into the bag and to feel the object. Ask him to describe that object without saying what it is. Encourage the child to use words like 'rough', 'smooth', 'sharp edges' or 'crinkly'. Can the other children guess what it is?
- In the kitchen, make a collection of foods, in small dishes, such as salt, flour, sugar, butter, honey, cheese, raw carrot, cauliflower or potato, bread, cooked and uncooked pasta, baked beans and so on. Ask the children to touch and describe how the foods feel – hard, soft, squashy or sticky.
- Explain to the children that our skin feels pain through nerve endings. Ask them to run their fingers through their hair. How does that feel? Then ask them to pick up one hair and pull it. (Don't pull too hard!) Can they feel the pain when they pull their hair? This is because the nerve endings under the skin of our heads tell the brain that the skin is being pulled.
- Prepare some bowls of hot (not too hot), warm and cold water. (Add ice to make it really cold.) Ask the children to put their hand in the cold water and count to 20. Ask: Does the water seem as cold now? Then ask them to put their hand in the warm water. How does that feel? Experiment with going from hot to cold water/warm to cold/cold to hot.

Week 6 – Touch

Mathematical Development

 Use developing mathematical ideas and methods to solve practical problems.

Sorting

- Sort and categorise the kitchen equipment (see Knowledge and Understanding of the World). Sort by texture (rough or smooth) and temperature (warm or cold to touch).
- Model writing labels for the categories – for example, 'All these things are smooth.'

Make a bar graph

- Give each child a small square of paper and ask them to draw and label something in the role play area that is hard, soft, cold, and so on. Create a simple bar graph with the names of the categories given along the base. The children should stick their pictures in the correct column. Ask the children which column has the most items.

Extension

- Collect around 30 small objects from the kitchen, such as a spoon, a small storage box and a can opener. Ask the children to arrange the objects in three rows of ten and count the total in tens. Then ask them to put the objects in rows of five and count the total in fives (5, 10, 15…) Finally, show them how to record the numbers in a tally (𝐼𝐼𝐼𝐼 = 5).

Play games

- Challenge the children to touch something cold, warm, soft, hard, rough and smooth. The aim is to be first back to the teacher having followed the instructions.

Communication, Language and Literacy

 Use a pencil and hold it effectively.

Pencil control

- Give each child a pencil and paper. Show them how to make light and dark marks on the paper by pressing lightly and firmly. Ask them to take their pencil for a walk over the paper, sometimes pressing lightly, sometimes pressing hard. Look at the patterns they have made. Ask them to write their name, first pressing lightly and then pressing firmly.

Speaking and listening

- Revisit the texts explored during this unit. Which did the children like best? Are there any images they particularly remember or any facts they can recall? Make a list of these facts under the heading 'We have learned …'
- Share with the children the poems on page 35.

Singing

- Sing 'A feely game' or 'A hedgehog is very prickly' from *Bobby Shaftoe Clap Your Hands*. (See Resources)

Writing labels

- Remind the children how to make labels. Give each child a different texture to feel – for example, hard, soft, smooth, rough (see Mathematical Development). Encourage them to make labels for each texture.

Week 6 – Touch

Supported writing

❏ Develop the labels created earlier into sentences. Orally rehearse the sentences with the children (for example, 'This fabric feels smooth,', 'This material feels rough,') and then encourage them to write them down. For less confident children, ask them to dictate what they want written. Demonstrate writing the sentence in highlighter pen and ask the children to write inside the highlighter writing.

Extension

❏ Support the children as they write up some of their experiments (see Knowledge and Understanding of the World). Model the frame for the children – for example, 'When I put my hand in the feely bag…'

Creative Development

 Explore colour, texture, shape and form in two or three dimensions.

Ready, steady, cook

❏ Provide some play dough, knives, rolling pins and cutters. Ask the children to make a variety of food. Talk about the appearance of sandwiches or little cakes with a cherry on the top. Encourage them to arrange their food neatly on individual plates.

Make a soft toy

❏ Prepare for each child two fur fabric or felt templates of a cat or a teddy, some lengths of pipe cleaner for whiskers and a tail, and some white and black felt rounds for eyes. With adult support, encourage the children to sew, using a simple running stitch, around the edge. (Knotted, double thread is easiest to work with.) More able children can try to thread their own needles. Then the children can go back along the seams the other way. Leave a gap of at least 6cm so that the toy can be stuffed. Stuff with old cut-up tights or fabric scraps and sew to finish. Add the whiskers (sewn or glued) and the eyes (sewn or glued) out of felt. NB: use a piece of doweling or a wooden spoon to push the stuffing into the toy.

Toys party

❏ Hold a toys' party in the role play area where the children serve their play food to their soft toy.

Physical Development

 Use a range of large and small equipment. Move in confidence and safety.

Music and movement

❏ Sing the hokey cokey with all the actions.

Play a listening game

❏ Ask the children to sit in a circle facing inwards. Spread out in the centre of the circle a selection of hard, soft, smooth, rough and silky objects. Number the children one to four. Call a number – for example, two. All those given the number two get ready to move. Call out a description of the feel of an object in the circle – for example, something furry. The children stand up, run round the circle, back through their space into the centre, pick up the correct object and race to be first to give it to you. Be careful to spread the objects in the centre in order to avoid accidents!

Gymnastics

❏ When using mats and benches, encourage the children to experiment with using different parts of the body when travelling. Can they feel which parts of their body are touching the apparatus or the floor?

Review and evaluation

Encourage the children to reflect on the topic. What have they enjoyed learning about? Which part has been most exciting? Which stories and songs do they remember? Which artwork did they most enjoy doing?

Poems and songs 1

My brother

He giggles and squeaks,
And curls and rolls,
And wriggles and cries,
And screws up his eyes,
And squirms and squeals
And shouts and yells,
And screeches and begs,
And kicks his legs,
Till Mum puts her head
Round the door and says
'Stop tickling your brother!'

Theresa Heine

Oh Baby!

Ever since the baby came
Life at home is not the same,
Of course, my friends and I were not
Supposed to breathe in case he woke,
And playing silently's no joke.
We soon found out why all the fuss –
The baby made more noise than us!

Then at mealtimes from his chair
He threw his dinner everywhere –
Peas and ham went whizzing by,
Soggy custard, apple pie –
My dad and I soon learned to duck,
My mother said, 'With any luck,
He'll soon be past this stage and then
We'll all enjoy our food again.'

He's talking now and drives me dotty
Shuffling round me on his potty,
Wanting me to stay and play,
Repeating everything I say –
Though I'm not too certain
Just what it is about him,
Despite his crazy antics,
I wouldn't be without him.

June Crebbin

Potty, but True

My little baby sister
Spends hours on the pot,
Smiling on her plastic throne – but she
doesn't do a lot.

Mum and Dad sit waiting
While baby sister wriggles;
But she produces nothing,
Except some burps and giggles.

Mum and Dad look worried,
It shows up all their wrinkles;
But still my little sister
Just won't provide those tinkles.

Mum and Dad try very hard,
They always promise treats;
If she would only fill the pot
They'd buy her toys and sweets.

But I could tell them something
They really ought to know;
The second that she's off the pot
That's when she's bound to go!

Tony Bradman

Tiny little fingernails

Tiny little fingernails, tiny little toes
Tiny little hands and tiny little nose
That's how I started out to be
But now I'm bigger, just look at me!
We are growing as children do
And soon we will be bigger than you!

Tiny little ears and tiny little cheeks
Tiny little knees and tiny little feet
That's how I started out to be
But now I'm bigger, just look at me!
We are growing as children do
And soon we will be bigger than you!

Niki Davies

Poems and songs 2

What are friends like?

Friends are kind
Friends are fun
Friends can talk and listen too,
Friends can help
Friends can hug
You like them and they like you.

Friends can share
Friends can care
Friends can play with you all day,
Friends say sorry
Friends forgive
Friends don't sulk or run away.

Friends are good
Friends are great
Friends can laugh and joke with you,
Friends are true
Friends are fond
Friends enjoy the things you do
I like friends, don't you?

Ruth Kirtley

Today for lunch

Today for lunch I had –
10 sizzling spoonfuls of specially spiced soup,
9 beautiful bites of brown baked bread,
8 chewy chunks of crispy, crinkly chips,
7 black bits of burnt baked beans,
6 terrific titbits of tasty tender tomatoes,
5 fat fingers of freshly fried fish,
4 pleasing pieces of perfect pecan pie,
3 creamy cups of cool clotted cream
2 jumbo jars of juicy jolly jelly
Which left me with
1 big bulge of bursting burping belly!

Ian Souter

Me and you

Oh, I've got one head,
And one nose too,
One mouth and one chin
And so have you.
Oh, I've got two eyes
And two ears too,
Two legs, two arms
And so have you.
Oh, I've got two thumbs
And so have you.

Anon

My eyes can see

My eyes can see.
(Make spectacles with hands.)

My mouth can talk.
(Bring index finger down on thumb repeatedly.)

My ears can hear.
(Cup hand, put behind ear.)

My feet can walk.
(Palms down, wriggle 2nd and 3rd fingers.)

My nose can smell.
(Touch nose with fingertip.)

My teeth can bite.
(Palms together, move fingertips together and back.)

My eyelids can flutter.
(Hold hands close to eyes, move fingers up and down.)

My hands can write.
(Pretend to hold a pencil.)

Anon

Poems and songs 3

After my bath

After my bath
I try, try, try
To wipe myself
Till I'm dry, dry, dry.

Hands to wipe
And fingers and toes
And two wet legs
And a shiny nose.

Just think how much
Less time I'd take
If I were a dog
And could shake, shake, shake.

Aileen Fisher

Clap your hands

Clap your hands, clap your hands,
Clap them just like me.
Touch your shoulders, touch your shoulders,
Touch them just like me.
Tap your knees, tap your knees,
Tap them just like me.
Shake your head, shake your head,
Shake it just like me.
Clap your hands, clap your hands,
Now let them quiet be.

Anon

Hands up

Hands to the ceiling
Hands touch the floor,
Reach up again,
Let's do some more.
Now touch your head,
Then touch your knee,
Then touch your shoulder,
Just like me.
Hands to the ceiling,
Hands touch the floor.
That's all for now, goodbye –
There isn't any more.

Anon

Sight

I asked a little boy who cannot see,
'And what is colour like?'
'Why green,' said he,
'Is like the rustle when the wind blows through
The forest; running water, that is blue;
And red is like a trumpet sound; and pink
Is like the smell of roses; and I think
That purple must be like a thunderstorm;
And yellow is like something warm;
And white is a pleasant stillness when you lie
And dream.'

Making things

1. Making a changing table

- You will need a large cardboard box.
- Either turn it inside out, re-form and glue together again, or cover with suitable paper.
- Ask the children to choose a colour to paint the box.
- When dry, use suitable paint and print patterns on the box using corks, cotton reels, Stickle bricks, Unifix cubes or Lego pieces.
- Place the box in the nursery. Put a folded blanket or towel on top as a changing mat. Place a basket containing cotton wool balls, empty 'baby cream' pots (labelled) (see Communication, Language and Literacy), nappies and an empty talcum powder container on the changing table.

2. Making a cot

- You will need a large cardboard box.
- Either turn it inside out, re-form and glue together again, or cover with white paper.
- Ask the children to paint stripes on the outside to represent the bars of the cot. Decorate the inside, printing patterns as above. Place a blanket or shawl in the cot.

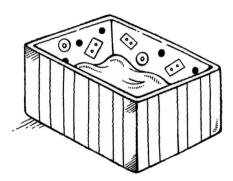

3. Making a rattle

- Provide a selection of small containers such as yogurt pots, plastic water bottles and cardboard tubes.
- Provide a selection of dried peas, lentils and beans.
- Show the children how to fill a yogurt pot with lentils and tape another pot on top to seal.
- Show the children how to seal the end of a tube or a container with card and masking tape. (Make a card shape a little larger than the open end of the container. Snip around the edge of the card. Folding the snipped edges over the open end, tape the card to the container.)
- Provide paints, scraps of brightly coloured paper and glue for the children to decorate their rattles.

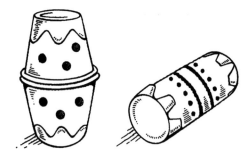

Safety note

Stress to the children that they should never use any of these things with a real baby, as they are not safe; especially the rattle which could choke a child.

Handwriting

Starting with role play

A jam sandwich

Making a jam sandwich

You will need:
a loaf
jam
margarine
knife

What to do:

Cut two slices of bread.

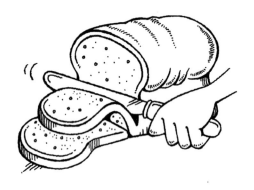

Spread margarine on the bread.

Spread jam on the bread.

Put the slices of bread together and cut into four pieces.

Signs

Starting with role play

Observational Assessment Chart

Unit: _____ Class: _____ Date: _____

Name	Personal, Social and Emotional Development	Communication, Language and Literacy	Knowledge & Understanding of the World	Mathematical Development	Creative Development	Physical Development
	Y B G ELG	Y B G ELG	Y B G ELG	Y B G ELG	Y B G ELG	Y B G ELG
	Y B G ELG	Y B G ELG	Y B G ELG	Y B G ELG	Y B G ELG	Y B G ELG
	Y B G ELG	Y B G ELG	Y B G ELG	Y B G ELG	Y B G ELG	Y B G ELG
	Y B G ELG	Y B G ELG	Y B G ELG	Y B G ELG	Y B G ELG	Y B G ELG
	Y B G ELG	Y B G ELG	Y B G ELG	Y B G ELG	Y B G ELG	Y B G ELG
	Y B G ELG	Y B G ELG	Y B G ELG	Y B G ELG	Y B G ELG	Y B G ELG
	Y B G ELG	Y B G ELG	Y B G ELG	Y B G ELG	Y B G ELG	Y B G ELG
	Y B G ELG	Y B G ELG	Y B G ELG	Y B G ELG	Y B G ELG	Y B G ELG
	Y B G ELG	Y B G ELG	Y B G ELG	Y B G ELG	Y B G ELG	Y B G ELG
	Y B G ELG	Y B G ELG	Y B G ELG	Y B G ELG	Y B G ELG	Y B G ELG
	Y B G ELG	Y B G ELG	Y B G ELG	Y B G ELG	Y B G ELG	Y B G ELG
	Y B G ELG	Y B G ELG	Y B G ELG	Y B G ELG	Y B G ELG	Y B G ELG

Circle the relevant Stepping Stones (Y = Yellow; B = Blue; G = Green or ELG = Early Learning Goal) and write a positive comment as evidence of achievement.